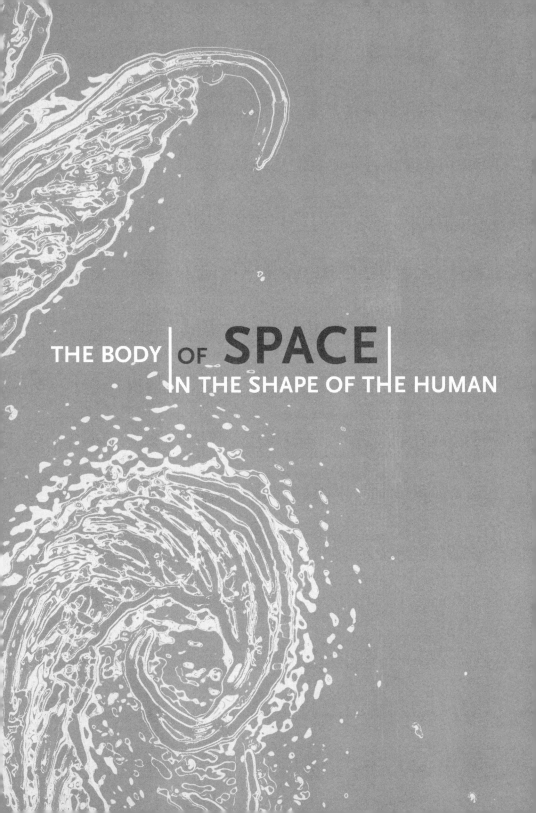

THE BODY OF **SPACE** IN THE SHAPE OF THE HUMAN

New Issues Poetry & Prose

Editor   William Olsen

Guest Editor   Nancy Eimers

Managing Editor   Kimberly Kolbe

Layout Editor   Elizabyth A. Hiscox

Assistant Editor   Traci Brimhall

New Issues Poetry & Prose
The College of Arts and Sciences
Western Michigan University
Kalamazoo, MI 49008

First Edition, 2012.

ISBN-13   978-1-936970-05-6 (paperbound)

Library of Congress Cataloging-in-Publication Data:
Allport, Andrew
the body | of space | in the shape of the human/Andrew Allport
Library of Congress Control Number: 2011943415

Art Director   Ern Bernhardi
Designer   Sara Annela Tomeo
Production Manager   Paul Sizer
                      The Design Center, Frostic School of Art
                      College of Fine Arts
                      Western Michigan University
Printing   McNaughton & Gunn, Inc.

THE BODY | OF **SPACE**|
IN THE SHAPE OF THE HUMAN

ANDREW ALLPORT

New Issues Press

WESTERN MICHIGAN UNIVERSITY

For Diana | of course

Contents

IV.

Acknowledgements

Grateful acknowledgement is made to the editors of the publications in which the following poems appeared:

Antioch Review | "Meditation Ending with a Line from Celan"

Blackbird | "Chronos", "Keats, Climbing", "Sarcophagus"

Boston Review | "In a Peaceful Place"

Crate | "The Professions of St. Augustine"

Colorado Review | "Postscript"

Denver Quarterly | "Post-Tempest," "Don't Write at All," "The Papermakers"

The Los Angeles Review | "Purgatorio"

The Offending Adam | "A Bed above the Abyss: Amnesiac Notebook"

ZYZZYVA | "An Unknown Shore: Variations on a Fragment by Oppen"

The poems "An Unknown Shore" and "Keats, Listening to Van Morrison" appeared in the 2010 anthology *The Loudest Voice* (Figueroa Press), a publication of the Los Angeles reading series by the same name. "An Unknown Shore" also appeared in the anthology *Best New Poets 2006* (Samovar Press, 2006). Many of these poems were first published in the chapbook *The Ice Ship & Other Vessels*, which won the 2008 Proem Press award.

Thank you to everyone who has helped with these poems. And to family and friends who have supported and encouraged me—this book is for you, too.

I.

Gloucester. *When shall I come to th' top of that same hill?*
Edgar. *You do climb it now. Look, how we labor.*

—King Lear, IV.6

Horrible Steep

Gloucester. *Methinks the ground is even.*

Feel the cold spray of stars on your cheek,
  taste the sliver of moonlight
    gouged from its case. How horrible
    orbital the ground, how lonely the shivering

cries of coyotes, the dry wind called oblivion sweeping
  the ridge's familiar silhouettes of rock:
    the Old Woman's long face, the Headstone
    crowned with stars. At the end's edge, the cliff writes

its own description of the ships, the tiny lights, your life
  startling an owl from a branch above—
    caesura of breath, then I begin as actor, an Edgar
    in the howling manner of a beggar

draping the space of your body
in false report, a coat of wings.

Chronos

You left no space untouched, uneaten.

Sliding the knife like a zipper from anus

to the base of the jaws, you opened

the fish, you went in head first, biting

eggs from their bed. *It's caviar,* you said,

it's gravy. What a stroke of luck, what wild

fortune, O string of globes found in the folds.

You went in and your flannel was silver

with scales, and when you arose the fish

was upon your shoulders, the hybrid father

of the riddle, waving the thin knife,

you worked the hinge of the jaw

pretending to offer of yourself: *Eat me,*

the fish says, *or I you.* The fish in pursuit,

its callused hands lifting its roe

to my mouth: *eat, eat,* the rank ocean

bursts on my tongue. *It only feels*

like a choice, I tell myself, tightening

your watch on my wrist, looking in the glass:

I am wearing your head, watching my hands

zip up your jacket. When I scattered

sand of your flesh, the sea was gone

a moment, a million years.

Purgatorio

non per vista, ma per suono é noto (Inferno, XXXIV)

I spent a year there, searching for the right line,
trying to translate that long silence
into sight: neither darkness nor brightness

but snow falling on snow, the radio losing strength
in the tunnel. Even static has its edges, its windows.
Even the truth can be dressed in curtains, trees, a forest,

a fortress: inside, my mountain was pathetic:
man-made, catastrophic, it could hardly bear
weight, its summiteers barely cared if I blessed

or damned them. I did not imagine a tragedy
would be so full of extras, spinning chairlifts,
ascending without effort into the empyrean,

or that the weather would be so mild. Winter, spring:
in an unconsolidated space nothing connects
with nothing, and you slide from scene to scene.

I pick up a red paging phone and am shocked
with news: the king went early to his idyll, died
with a smile on his face. The archetypes will not

hold, I heard the radio say, I heard the first canto
of avalanche safety say the odds are zero, oh, o, o, o
and our job is recovery, not rescue.

So I spent a January sun, shovel and probe in hand,
close-reading snow: beacon calls out, bat-blind, to
the body: you're getting colder, colder, no—now you're hot,

hotter, you're so hot you're on fire, you're burning—
and there it was. A face, encased in a second face,
a mask of ice, his breath. In an unconsolidated space,

death is half the story. We wrapped him in silver,
laid him in the litter. A numb remembrance
of the knots remains at hand. It was all by the book:

the sled, the rope, the weight, the boots.
The world read into, each object animated
by the same unbelievable sight, indelible

as the range of light: the calm town of stone
where we gather each spring around the marker we made,
we made it resemble (how could we not) a mountain.

And on the Third Day

We called off the search,
and the weary climbed down from the glacier
with their dogs exhausted in the spring sun
too tired to eat the ice in their paws.

We had called his name, mostly for show,
a ritual that kept us moving: in the high bowls,
their stunted pines predating the flood,
in the steep ravines sliding loose with scree,
loudly at first, then speaking it to each other
then spelling it out on forms required by law.

It is a form of praying, he claimed, to walk
out to the very edge of your life. Every time
the reply comes clear as a stone
at our thin crowns. It misses
almost every time, humming as it goes.

In a Peaceful Place

A poem of unmediated experience
begins a poem of unmediated experience.

I came to sprawled in the stiff white grass
of the shoulder, and they said stay still.

I came to, and they said hello again. A poem begins,
do you know what day it is?

What a tiny target, an aspirin strung on fishing line.
What a giant moon above the Arno. Ah Florence!
like a land of dreams before them, a poem begins.

Please obey the poetics of indeterminacy,
the grammar of silence.
The poetics of indeterminacy are.

Unfolding the moon is a mistake.
I still recall is a mistake. The likeness
of our bodies is a mistake—

Your name is, they began. Your phone.
It was the scene of someone's accident—
my heart went out to him.

My Father's Reel

My father the murderer
My father the gangster
My father the judge

He dies in a shootout
He dies in a plane crash
He dies with his men

At the hands of monsters
He came from the future
He was set in the past

He returns from the war
with a limp, a wooden cane
he discards to dance

And now he pretends to swim
acting the backstroke in air
he has gone through the window
in a rain of sugar glass

The key to the mystery
He confesses to the crime
I'll see you, he says. And he does,
unreal, lasting, light as a prop

held aloft with the expression—
I trust it—that inclination of arm,
reluctance of the hand—of weight

My father driving the new car
My father calling toll-free
My father who may be at risk

My father haunting his wife
My father robbed of dignity
My father *a man may see how this world goes*
My father *with no eyes*

The Pass

What good fortune brought you to this
pass then passed. What blind eye was turned
inward, what luck lucked out and paid off
in spades, what crooked marker bade
turn here where between white slopes
white shadows slide and rise. And what sound
or silence arose from that last arc you drew
across the face of the snow, what crack
or smile widened into laughter, whose
shape crossed beneath your feet as water
in one form and then another gathered.
What mix of breath and vapor escaped
what unheard melody. I heard them express
at the service what an encompassing
embrace, what passion. What person
is left greeting the long line of what ifs.

Off Great Point

In a room of changing light we let the island

wash away. I saw a steeple in the rip where waves

met over the sandbar, a ripple where the bone lands

amid the ash, a wake made by we who live to cast

for blues. A cloud overhead broken into branches

by the chop, slapping the hull, dash these our last

remarks—here the minister arose to say he died

as a boy, only to awake on shore, and never swam again.

There are no trees here, he intoned, since they became

the boats: there are no trees here on our island,

only spaces that might have been. As though these

shadows might be assembled, float.

At the Courthouse

The forms are pink, yellow, blue—
salmon, canary, bluebell—
or birth, marriage, death

flowering in the waiting room.
Outside the building cars creep on a cloverleaf,
that knot of road built to wish us well.

Good luck, little fish.
Inside, we have nothing
to swim but time and anger.

Look, someone says—
but the hawk in the atrium's tree
is gone. Try again, she says

at the window, handing me a better pen.
Hard as I press,
the copy underneath (the one

"to keep") stays a blank blue sea.
On the sixteenth floor, salmon leap,
a canary sings in the bluebells—

and from a door down the hall,
someone will emerge soon
with the form to record it all.

Postscript

Think of the moon, the rest of it. Singing,
a new bird began outside my window
to encircle my sleep with a song like spring,
ripeness overtaking the green. Awake,

I wished for the visions I hear are going around:
the dead returning to stroke my hand, open
my eyes to their voices' inaudible music,
the negative version of the gaunt moon,

an itch in my shoulders where the wings sprout
at the sound of song, a benediction from legibility.
Then a plume of guilt, knowing there is nothing
I don't form through the reach of writing

your last words, the final note still missing,
your song without end (forgive me) I end.

II.

"My good doctor," he exclaimed, "in the history of the world there is no such thing as going back!"
—Musil, *The Man Without Qualities*

The Oblivion Pact

Nothing recorded,   nothing recalled—
I shook   his hand and showed the palm—
nothing held,   nothing harmed

our smiles gun   another boy down
who had it coming.   The future
we will build it   will build
his memorial   ourselves

a river is all   we need
to forget   these past lives
its mouth   empties teeth and bone

our handshake   rises up and fells
an axe through   knots of tendon.

The war has been   important to anatomy
the doctor says   our understanding
of phantom limbs   has grown

He says   Nothing
can come   after nothing—
true, but not   for long

Post-Tempest

Consider the *blue*, formerly *blewe*
skye, still the *bleween*, *blowne*
skye, the sky from which
clouds are *blown*,
dispersed.

Consider the *blue sea*, formerly *blewe*
sae which contains placid *zee*,
and perilous *sjar*, the tempestuous sea
on whose shore emerges
our empire of
anachronism.

When we lay down in the field
flowers Shakespeare called *chimneysweeps*
waved their solemn clocks.
The sky had changed
when we woke unable
to name this feeling:

a new *breeze*
come from Portugal,
or the familiar *scythe*
lifting the white globes
out of sight.

The Papermakers

Art older than Christ, its rags more colorful,
its watermark two hands open to receive a gift:

a piece of silver, a blank check, the universal sign
for alms. During the weeping, the hand-wringing,

wet pages began falling, leafing through saturated air
curling around survivors' arms as they wilted

under the white heat of the sky dome.
In the exposed roots of the oaks, in the rigging of boats

sunk in their berths, upon the archipelago
of rooftops, an endless supply of fresh sheets

tiling the muddy water, delicate flagstones
offering the solace of the idea of disaster

as a clean page, a baptismal current of paper,
God's great pulpy torrent ripping,

running bodies through a sieve of cyclone fence.
So we pinned the first page to the first found:

art older than Christ, finding something
to write with and on at the insistence of the dead.

The Late Address of Captain Shane T. Adcock

o

Today I am consecrated, yet I would rather be anything
but king today—I would chew through this plastic bag to feel
a solitary drop of rain dampen my remains—
killed and redeemed by a button, a white glove,
an honor guard flanking my caisson, whose wheels weep.

o

My widow, a black blossom opening—

o

I have no shield, no solace, no uniform,
only the brass buttons my eyes have become,
the formal silver of bit and bridle—
today I am among regal animals, a militia of angels:
my forefathers' eyes bled through cornhusk bandages at Antietam,
watched the yellow silk fly on San Juan hill, checked the battleship's clock
every quarter hour. Grandfather, who taught me Norfolk time—
eight bells and all's well—by the Tigris they tore your watch from my wrist.

o

We never know when light will hit us next,
we who endowed with nightvision no longer press ears to the ground
or noses to the air, but flatten the mountains to maps,
light into lasers, roll along the hard road like a ball inside a ball,
unaware that its own revolution may be contrary to its direction.
No event ever stops spinning, despite our efforts the hands can't grasp
or push out of mind the slow rise of the spirit,
the falling of the bucket, the washed-out sky, a vision
seen from the bottom of a well.

o

The bucket brings up sand, the wells are fiery columns
supporting a palace of smoke and charred air—
these late eclipses of the sun and moon portend no good to us,
our intent eclipsed by incident, our knowledge appearing only in outline,
decorated by its absence. Dismissed from life by a Reason,
I had class, civility, and a beautiful eye.

o

                              She can't forget
how she forgets. The people I resembled have changed—
lost my detail, my currency, converted to a small round coin
thrown into the fountain of grief. In her dream, she is racing away
from a runaway caisson, and it crushes her.

o

I am almost gone, yet engraved here in the earth,
tally and tower, wheel and whetstone for a sharpening darkness.
A blade trenches the ground, and names pass through its wound,
casting their shades like the noise of invisible planes, a sound
heard underneath a thousand others.

o

The long note of a trumpet, dampened by rain.

Foreman

In the box were the victim's garments, stiff with blood.
He had been hogtied with duct tape,
silver bands still shone at wrist and ankle—

now we have to wear them, said the foreman,

so we did, one by one stepping inside
until the shirt billowed like a great red tent
as we held it overhead with our palms,
and the pants were like two long hallways
we walked for days between our verdict,

and as we gathered at the round table
we began to forget who we were
on the outside, each name lost to the eraser
of days passing through the courtroom—

until a show of hands was called for, said the foreman,
and we did, one by one, each empty, shackled to the other.

Patterns of Grace

Eighty bells, each decaying slower
　　　　　than the last—or so it seems
in the taut silence of the church,

a human silence, broken by coughs
　　　　　and the reverend microphone
still live, overdriven by heavy breathing.

Smoke was your last love, you said
　　　　　between trips to the oxygen
bank, where they coaxed back to pink

your fragile barrel chest swollen
　　　　　by emphysema, you told me
isn't it a gas, you weighed a year

against French cigarettes and came down
　　　　　lightly, with hardly a sound.
The diaphragm in one speaker's blown; fuzz

clips the breath and the bells decay
　　　　　patterns, it seems, tolling twin
columns above us in the moment of—

—though we say breathing we mean
　　　　　inhaling, forgetting
expiration's churchlit peal, amplified.

A Bed above the Abyss: Amnesiac Notebook

i. Awake

Each entry consisting of the statements
I am awake or *I am conscious*
entered every few minutes:

> *2:10 p.m.: this time properly awake.*
> *2:14 p.m.: this time finally awake.*
> *2:35 p.m.: this time completely awake.*

> *At 9:40 p.m. I awoke for the first time, despite my previous claims.*

This in turn was crossed out, followed by:

> *I was fully conscious at 10:35 p.m., and awake for the first time*
> *in many, many weeks.*

This in turn was cancelled out by the next entry.

ii. Passport

How large it grew, that first kiss, until I could board it each night,
a raft drifting out into the quiet lake. After twenty years
the great amnesiac HM never recognized
his doctor, and after lunch
gladly ate another: Time for lunch, they would tell him again.
You must be starving.

God, I *am* starving.
Without a body, collection cannot precede
recollection: recollect a tongue, that skilled swirl
of its quick tip, a mouthful of familiars: smoke,
strawberry candy. Memory in the web
between dumbstruck and dura: dump and dune,
duplicates. What kind of game is this?

I'm no longer a boy,
HM would say to his reflection, the surprise on his face
genuine. What kind of game *is* this?
The mirror a passport like any other, its picture
out of time, a foreign shock of untamed hair
even the photographer declared beautiful then.

Then: the word smiles
like a stranger on your first day at school,
sitting on stone steps, worn with use.

iii. Taxonomy

"*Red* but not *bird* comes to mind."
              Only the kingdom of living names

was missing there—bank, flagstone, sofa
              remained, but not the blur at the feeder,

the undersea creature on the card—
              it's a danger, a killer swimmer,

they coaxed him—it's called a
              (waiting for the word to stir from its depth;

how could he forget the ones who dressed,
              fed, taught him word by word

the order of the world? What noise does
              that loss make?) (They looked suspiciously

like his parents, he thought: strangers posing
              unanswerable questions)—

"It has no name, it has no need."

Poem Ending with an Icepick Lobotomy

Laid out in a white envelope,
I heard his bone hammer,

the tapered orbitoclast
a silver letter opener

sliding between gummed flaps,
a crack of daylight between hollow

and tissue, an entrance of instrument,
the bulbs smashed in their sockets.

Lions, water, the dark—
they said I was scared of everything

unreal. Even then, informally arranged
on the dining table, I admit

to dreaming
when the dull pencil intruded.

Nights, I have been to the river,
I have seen the eyes of lions

bright with menace.
Then I lay on the bank,

counting stars.
Then there were none.

An Unknown Shore: Variations on a Fragment by Oppen

Cortez arrives.
                  he is absolutely lost
at an unknown shore.
                  and he is enraptured

(this is the nature of poetry

The poem:

Cortez arrives at an unknown shore
 he is absolutely lost
 and he is enraptured

Cortez arrives at an unknown shore
 he is utterly lost
 but he is enraptured

Cortez arrives too late.
 the shore is absolutely barren, the men lost
         to starvation and rapture

Cortez utters:
 "lost."

(this is the nature of description

Cortez walks upon the beach.
 the ocean is as still as a map
 spread out on a table.

 (he takes a nap.

Cortez arrives, sun-senseless (?
 wrapped in gold
 ~~plashing in the shallow~~

 All the Cortezs arrive.
 all the waves arrive

 (this is the nature of disaster

III.

They contemplate nothing but parts, and all parts are necessarily little!—the universe to them is but a mass of little things.
—Coleridge, *Letter to Poole*, 10/16/97

What Would Come to Be Known as The Years of Confusion

In those days no name was given to the abyss
        beyond the year's end.
The unnumbered next thing lay fallow

while in the razed fields we paused to shine
        our blades
until the first march of the new campaign,

our "state of permanent pre-hostility" lasting
        sixty suns.
Even the emperor quieted His hands, wherein

holding a thousand means for seizing
        open terrain.
Hours were marked by the state of mud.

That time can be wasted is imperial
        thought: the void
in which no god reigns, this calendar of disorder

should be righted, he mused, crossing the border
        in January,
early autumn of the last so-called year of confusion.

Now I wade through the last Tuesday of February,
        2008: last year
of the echo dynasty, and all questions asked of legacy:

Will the deeds of the son outpace his father's
        and if so
whose face will they impress on the coin first,

whose name will replace the season? Co-workers
                    ask how I am
these days: stuck like a specimen between tomorrow

and yesterday, the present recedes like the surface of a lake—
                    they stop asking.
The emperor trusted the algorithm with perpetuity

and made of the summer a monument to his son.
                    I think of the rocks
I lifted into place over your shoes disappearing

in a week's light traffic of barefoot ghosts
                    bearing resemblance
to my new self, vacant and thin as a mandolin.

The emperor is said to have hesitated at the river.
                    Then, music
from the other side: a god-like figure playing the pipes

and his men began to sing: how auspicious,
                    he thought,
a flock has formed an hourglass in the air.

Don't Write at All

Today the commencement of yearly rites.
Today a blimp overhead.
Today the brass tacks, the clean sheets.

Today the difficult poses: Bird of Paradise,
Standing Half-Moon, Flowering Wheel.
At the Buddhist retreat in Idyllwild
a man walks slowly back from breakfast.

He has missed lunch he is so slow.
Flies gather all over him.

A fly which Buddha forbids killing
crawls deep into his ear,
rippling the clear surface of his mantra.
A fly explores the pitted stone of his brain.

Today the intrusion of fireworks, the traded insults.
Today the sharp knuckle.
Today the hair-trigger, the shirtless boy
ready to burst in the heat, flying downcourt
in jeans loose as robes, leaping into white space

between obscenities. What today
is killed on the page still survives
in the world where no one reads.

The Professions of St. Augustine

i. Of Love & Language

I wanted to carry out | my inner lack | of feeling | which I had in plenty | I
sought | the excitement of | color | to shake | and carry off the | night |
what was | at the bottom of | my heart | let my heart tell | I loved my | self
| down from | firmament to ruin | for its own sake | There is beauty in |
such things | the body touches | much significance attaches | the other
senses | have their own | urge to self-assertion | one must not depart
from | this world | in its beauty and its | objects | of love and | language

ii. Of Flesh & Blood

ship | secretly | weeping | to sail | I | then asked, | prayed for | make
me | shore | lost to our sight | The wind blew | nations and groans |
ambitious desires | an end to | flesh and blood | a means of | lament |
remnants of | me and | home. | the longing | to use my absence |
survived | And yet after | I came to Rome | bearing all | against myself |
the | disposition to | deliver me from | the death of | flesh | I was |
numerous and serious | forgiven | delivered | contracted by my | flesh |
insofar as | my soul | was marked by all-night dancing.

iii. Of Limited Humanity

suffering so long from | certainty | I should have knocked | to discover | more painfully | uncertain things | you made humanity | whole and never limited | no bodily | head to foot | shame | they were certain | it was certain | as certain when | against you | I was being" "the body | of space | in the shape of the human | all sides and confined | the old writing | looked absurd, | with an eye | to attack | The letter | the mystical veil | difficulty; | I kept my heart

iv. Of Childish Error

our physical shape | limited to | Being ignorant | as an infant |
bounded on all sides | from head to foot | with blind accusations |
being turned around | as if they thought | the spirit gives life | within
the shape of the human | uncertain and | infantile | attack | I had
mindlessly repeated | Christ's | childish error | My concern to discover
what | did not hold | an infant | taken literally, seemed to contain |
promises of certainty | I was confused | I was also pleased | when
the old writings | most carefully enunciating a principle | a vast
and huge space | of exegesis: | the letter kills | what I could
hold for certain

v. Of an Empty Office

we were mistaken in | our pupils | we hesitate to knock at | the shape
of a human body | Great hope | by allowing | the soul | vain and empty
office | to pay | our problem | But put aside | significance | set aside |
the deity | in quality and in quantity | the body's | the soul's | small
sweetness | Death itself | a question | it may suddenly carry us off

Apology Adorned with a Stunned Sparrow

> *I observed that the very fact they were poets made them think*
> *they had a perfect understanding of all other subjects, of which*
> *they were totally ignorant.*
> —Plato, *"The Apology"*

Perfect understanding
       is the poem
we can't write,

       despite our distance
from the subject.
       And yet we gather

experience into nests
       of likeness
and die inside. There is no

       outside the nest
(this is our philosophy)
       only the sound of *fitch*

and its synonymous flock:
       vetch, plait, polecat,
"to move in small spurts."

       Each is correct
(this is our problem)
       but like a city, we believe

only our own. When
       I heard her
pebbles on my window,

I didn't wonder
what kind of stone, nor
    blame the moon

for her figure, backlit
    in my memory.
Which means: I understand

    nothing, perfectly,
like an iron bell
    in the abandoned church

struck by a random bird:
    perfect, ignorant, music
unheard by its maker.

Elegy for a Stunt Horse

Venice, CA

Once I found your tooth, long as my finger, rounded
by a long life of browsing, a brown blade
in the garden, relic of the pasture
preceding the houses, the city
barely a dry rustle in the grass
rolling down to the sea.

In another age, the house was
a barn; the garden the barnyard
where they buried Muggins, *Greatest Show
Horse of a Generation*. The stone said
so, softly, sanded by shoes.
Mornin, Muggins, and off to school
I went, *Evenin, Muggins*, turning on
the television to watch the war.

They say an era, but they were days
at the time, revelations distinct
as bones. One night, the sound
of gunfire; another, geese huddled
in the alley, cackling. Like a bullet,
they had to land somewhere. Don't
wear blue in Oakwood, Muggins,
they'll skin you alive.

Flood lights rained from helicopters,
the streets were thick with feathers.
Goodbye, Muggins, and we fled
uphill, clutching a tooth, the city
gangs, its geese flying over the ring,
performing their stupendous
acts, balanced on the back of a galloping bay.

Attila the Hutt

We're all gonna be a lot thinner.
    —Han Solo

Because history is an enormous trash compactor
            we are stuck inside
    no one bone can be separated
            from the others,

no record or television set
            can be distinguished
    from the vellum and worsted stuff
            falling continually

into the open lid
            of a century in which the obsolete—
    opera, formal declarations of war—
            smash into courtly love poetry,

jewel cases. In this space
            ever shrinking
    empires meet and deform,
            fictional and historic

skylines are brought
            down by force
    to basic vertical and horizontal
            lines in a tension
    beautiful as long as it lasts, until
            you turn away
    and cannot. We worried

a loss of knowledge
            would make us dumb
    when an excess has the same effect,
            so many packages

the floor disappears,
        so many books
    the reader has no time to read
        but blankly watches

the walls now beginning to shift,
        making him the middle part
  of a trilogy he is compelled to follow

as it follows
        himself as himself
  barely recognizable.

Ode (with Fragments) on the Snowplant

i.

We're no Sapphos, simply saprophytes: not
able to use the sun's gift of bright intro-
spection. We can't synthesize, but can we
    solve this springy light?

I was green all season, I took photos by the
book—I stared down, deferential, at my future:
ground, until I tasted rotting underleaves, until you
    showed me how to trade

Death and Decay for the blood shade, O
negative, in your petal pulse. *Red life might
stream again, and thou be chloroformed—*
    Scarlet, I rebuke, it's a clever

Rouge, but it only works if you dye
all the way to the roots. What keeps us
blooming is the old material, not the mulchy
    promise of your mouth.

Nourished by rehashing old litter, you go
underground, cave in. Your sense of décor
lightens the mood with patterns, weaves,
    new camouflage.

Lyric tulips carpet your crypt, decorating
winter's wraparound wall. See—here you are,
snowbound, trying to make the heart's dead and dying
    matter matter:

ii.

*

No one captures more in their cape than you,
Hood: stem to stamen, you're right as Spring rain.

*

Winter's body, rehashed to pulp, hatches
hungry, giddy, ravenous, ?
stumbles across the dead landscape underfoot
   ricochet off trees

*

Shaggy scent of decay, mind's metaforgery

*

Spring's the time for sprouting things: verdure (root:
verd, from Obsolete French) vernal—see "Romantic
Ode to X"—you signify a bloomer, a bloody
   platter of hearts.

The Ice Ship

Pyke, from his Massachusetts madhouse,
        envisioned it
as a divine craft, an Ark impervious to torpedoes.

ICE is with us, ICE will win this war,
        he wrote
Mountbatten. With a draft of one hundred and fifty feet,

two million tons displacement, it could carry
        one hundred
twin-engine planes, three thousand men,

and required no steel to assemble,
        only water and pulp.
Onboard, the men lived in cork-paneled cabins,

skated down corridors to deliver urgent messages.
        A miracle ship,
organically arisen from the element

it moved in, indistinguishable from its medium,
        formed by Nature's design,
not the Royal Navy's, even her weaponry

resembled God's own: "brine guns" which
        encased the enemy
like straw in glass, machines that clogged harbors

with a flotilla of icebergs. Churchill played
        in his bath
with a model, and laughed, and ordered

White Bay to be drained, all the empire's cork
        diverted north
for a prototype built by Canadian COs.

It may be gold, it may only glitter—I have been hammering
          too long, and am blind.
It lasted into the spring, shedding coats

of sawdust, but by then the Allies were in
          France, while Mountbatten
threatening to commit him again

ignored a new plan for smuggling assassins
          into Berlin
in boxes marked "Officers Only"

on the grounds that Germans were an obedient race.
          Such are the dreams
war stirs, the rapture of slush, complete

complete dispersal of human forces into
          something larger:
ice is with us, and never leaves: that morning

he shaved his beard with asylum contraband:
          a little snowfall
had begun again, as his final view: the roof's

thick roof of snow, the blunted edges and cornices
          of the city,
a train in a train-sized clearing on the rails.   57

Cloud Effects: Variations on a Fragment by Coleridge

It was not a mist, nor quite a cloud
            but passed smoothly on towards the Sea
                        smoothly and lightly betwixt Earth & Heaven

so thin a cloud it scarce bedimmed the star that shone behind
            one blue-black cloud
                        stretched, like the heavens over all the cope of Heaven

                        a cloud upon which I had pinned all my hopes
I scarce recognized as a cloud

so threadbare and frayed yet still its own self
            discrete, as one cloud amid a mass of clouds
                        moves our eye to describe a figure amid other figures

a dose of clouds
            not a dream of clouds but a *dream cloud*

not the memory nor imagination but a cloud
            passing smoothly between them, and though I felt a shadow
                        looking up I could see no cloud
            neither here on Earth nor in Heaven nor in the in between

where an unwritten epic of clouds smoothly dissipates
            into imagination and the Sea and the one
                        whose Name casts a shadow over all names

IV.

Even in the center of his own essence, his enemy—nature, which is set in opposition to him—has established roots.
—Schlegel, *On the Study of Greek Poetry*

Wordsworth in the Sierra

Whose voice cries from the field of rock?

The still-born lamb, the excavating hawk:

each had his sky, each seemed the center

of his own fair world. Each morning, altitudinal light

needles the soul awake. Each evening, unhoused

beneath a flood of stars, the tallest peaks

are bathed in holy presence: one is the face

of a drowned man, another the blade of a skate.

On the white eye of a lake the poet

inches across, plunging through the snowcups,

leaving holes the size of eternity. That is,

a stream was heard underfoot, and never seen.

Wherein we might examine the resemblance of memory

to the falling column of water across the valley.

It does not move: we watch: it seems to move.

He would not have said *glacially*; soon no one will.

Comerado

In the dustlight of dusk, two white
egrets shine in a manure pond
beside the road.

Better close
your windows   *I give you my hand*

Their ancient Toyota quits
they know no one will stop

setting sun and hills: the hieroglyph
for lodging flashes blue, white.

father and son   walking
home across empty   fields

Shall we stick together

He worked in the calf houses
among animals unaware of mercy,
its tortured logic, its lack of streetlights.

We could see the dad seemed to be doing
what he could to reach his son.
But this stuff   you step in   it sucks you in.

Marshes enchain the base
of the foothills. I mean, once.
The air was clear. Perhaps
they had a chance.

Give me   your hand

Fireweed along the Angeles Crest

Relive, relive, relieve.
The erasure of heat, panic
of sparks—
this is not that

fire. Twisting rails,
a steel helix—
these are not those
flames. It is as it does: springs up, spreads, uncontained—

a touchable blaze, inviting
kin to the candle family.
Caught in its path,
a slope is pioneered with flower.

Revise, revise, reuse
the green fuse—
the weed stands
for all wounds: it adorns

the absence of the road,
absence of the house
with discretion:

unasked for, tacit. The sun
shines hardest here in the vacuum,
and no birds sing. No—one.   65

Keats, Listening to Van Morrison

Strange entanglement of singing, a twin voice

Stoned me like the nightingale

close enough it touched his ears then came closer, a vine

Stoned me like the hand missing arm

stretching out *I* into as many syllables as it pleases—

Stoned me like a god's lung, seared by song

but where does the air come from, when all is said

Stoned me like the exhale of a blue burden, bright red

at once, where does the breath go when it leaves?

Stoned me like the stone's imprint upon a lake

Sarcophagus

i.m. J.B., M.D., J.C., M.R.

1

Say I was there. I *was* there.
Only, a little after. Only, near.

Say I saw it. I *did* see. But not then, now.
Say I couldn't believe.

Say I couldn't believe
my eyes—they were a little late, say.

2

What began with a rock
falling, a flutter of a fist-sized piece

striking through the higher air, parting infinity:
as big as a breadbox

or a bookshelf, about the size of this desk
and of equal velocity to a feather:

3

: a wave, a wall, water vapor :
the outside rolls in : *blankets* as they say
   the scene or face : one coast slides under another

Somewhere the object continues
                  in spirit as they say
falling. Begin with this premise :

4

Ascending, and already that word seems
significant: pennies hammered edge-wise
in the grains of a downed fir
across the climber's trail—
what are they like, what do they stand for?
I do as I have done, always: touch them
for good luck, their shining edge.

5

Weekend chainsaws bray in the valley below
the white apron of stone called Suicide.

I climb into view of whatever Recorder
records these clear, conflicting desires:

Toby is climbing with a noose today
as a faith experiment. Legs elvising in fear,
inclined a degree beyond friction.

An Above exists, he tells me, moving up
delicately,
unbreakable as an eggshell.

6

What is solo   a single stone, a sol
economy of self   a light life (as in lifting)

A lone, as in reason   I went to the woods
deliberately to live   or to not. Of fears

what need one   reason   not the need
subtract from oneself   one

7

He stood on the boulder rising from the sea
imagining the word *whitecap* as a mountain in spring.

Is man less capable than a forest of kelp?
If all elements conspire to our delight,
Why should water drown its lord?

He stood in the mountain's mouth, thinking
how alike an avalanche to thunder.

8

The route index attests to divinity: Middle Cathedral, Angel's Wing.
The route index inclines toward evil: Devil's Tower, Devil's Thumb.
Our church is the church of the rock, he would say on Sundays.
It was true: a boulder had rolled through the apse, while the skyline
could be read diachronically as a hymn:
Awake, my soul and with the sun / my precious time misspent / redeem
The collective puzzle in parts, now joining (as in song)

9

It's a bathtub   exclaimed the boy   made out of rock
at the grave of the child   emperor   you sit down
it fills up   they shut it   and you swim

    The inscription reads   a bedtime story   here lies
    what was believed   an incarnation   a son
    two lives equally   mistaken   for a gulf

Aeolian

Two people in a room full of books
talking with their hands, sharing a grief
that is language.

Across the city, a hand uncurls
its fingers, plucking friend after friend
with news.

In one book, as long as we can say
this is the worst, we are wrong.

In another, each event is attended
by the unseen
agents of some larger cause,

and even the worst falls
fall to reason, in order
to stand for something.

In one book, air blows through
everything—
the paperweight is more comprehensible

than the paper. In another,
crickets have eaten away the margins,
a few choice phrases.

Keats, Climbing

The lost peak weighs heavy on him the weeklong trip
home from Fort William, its damp hand on his breastbone.
False summits, false ends, false altars of breath ascending
toward the sun, its old teeth gnawing at cloud-kept frost,
frigid mud engulfing each foot on the winding mudtrack.
The worst conditions in the world and only a whiskey muffler—
let this dram of gasping go down easy, a little gulp of fire
swing a censer between ribs—summits vaporating upon arrival,
summits sinking upon approach—as a dream destroyed
by grasping its tattered jacket, inurning what's left—
one ragged vision inside another, as the rinds of ruined lung
the surgeon excised, held: a wonder he breathed at all.

Meditation Ending with a Line from Celan

First empty the room of possessions.
Loaded into wheelbarrows beds

of busted chevys shopping bags
tied with rags onto horse & mule:

send each on its course.
Now don't move an inch, but leave

your mind stream like refugees
across the border of yourself. Try to make peace

close your eyes seeing only
your mantra scorched in the dark

floodlit. Then turn off the lights—
take out the bulbs.

Let your head be empty
as a crater filling with rainwater.

Picture yourself as the space
where a house once stood

a wind
blowing through the body's stubble field.

And after wind,   *the silence*
from which music may be born.

Canary

Gone crazy a little,
I hunt the house for something yellow.

Not in closets, drawers, cabinets.
Not on walls, floors, no trace in the white
paints, the smooth wood, the open sky.

No flower or vine in the greenery.
Neither lemon nor banana.
Not in the pens brimming over cups.

Surviving on snowmelt and juniper, the hermit
found himself with an appetite for mud,
his liver crying out for iron. He ate until
he drank, drank until he split open.

Craving without an outlet, pulling out wires,
checking each snake belly for a pale stripe.
The coward is connected to the ground:
the mind designs its reasons, then
shuts the bathroom door. Inside, I found
a late leaf, edged with red: some ending,
a doctor's circular message wound around a bottle.
Inside, the pills wait, a road edged with lights
between here and there, blinking caution.

Sonar

So near the skin you hear the blues,
swimming through your mother's ken.
There's the spine's wisp of smoke
the millimeter crust of bone rests
its globe upon. So far

some clouds obscure the continental body,
a cypress wrapped in fog.
The transceiver sweeps the room,
searching for the little swaddled

drum. When they found my father
buried in his pale cathedral, they said
he was having the time of his life,
that phrase exactly, so nearly true.
And yet. So far

our vision is a sound three times
beyond the highest note, a wave
your bones reflect. A snowy light veils
your face, perhaps a gift from him.

His hands were calm as ice, his eyes
fixed perfect. So near: see the corneas
nearly domed? *Which comparison does life begin*
I wonder—so near, there's the pulsing
star, there's the blizzard.

House, Home, Echo

I count them every evening, tiny fish
lit with phosphoresce, a school of lights
along the curving hilltop road
each house is a small globe
of incandescent fire where a mother
now sets down a plate of food before her child
so gently it does not make a sound
though the wind stirs its dark green border
of leaves. Later, they put out a little fire
and watch, and wait, and because I once lived
inside a house, I know that the one who enters
entertains one world with the other, swinging between
until the lock wears out with its turning
and the swinging motion of the door
becomes a hand stroking your back,
or waving in the crowd on the high deck
of a great ship, leaving for another country.

Notes

An Unknown Shore: Variations on a Fragment by Oppen:
The opening stanza comes from an unpublished series of
fragments included in *George Oppen: Selected Poems*
(New Directions, 2003).

The Late Address of Captain Shane T. Adcock: Captain Adcock,
27, of Mechanicsville, Virginia, died on October 11, 2006, in
Hawijah, Iraq. He was buried with full military honors in
Arlington National Cemetery.

Ode (with Fragments) on the Snowplant: The *sarcodes sanguinea*
appears in the Sierra Nevada mountains in the spring, pushing
its bright red stalk through the old snow. Lacking chlorophyll, it
lives by parasitizing the roots and decaying bodies of other
plants. The italicized line in this poem is from John Keats's
poem fragment "This living hand."

The Ice Ship: The best story of this episode is in David Lampe's
book, *Pyke, the Unknown Genius* (London: Evans Brothers, 1959).

The Professions of St. Augustine: All the language of this
poem is taken from Henry Chadwick's translation of
Augustine's *Confessions* (Oxford, 1991), and was composed
with Amaranth Borsuk.

Cloud Effects: Variations on a Fragment by Coleridge:
The fragments from Coleridge are found in *Anima Poetae*, a
collection of unpublished notebooks edited by Ernest Hartley
Coleridge (Cambridge: Riverside Press, 1895).

A Bed above the Abyss: Amnesiac Notebook: This poem is
indebted to Oliver Sacks' article, "The Abyss," which appeared
in *The New Yorker*, September 24, 2007.

Poem Ending with an Icepick Lobotomy: From 1936 to 1957, Dr. Walter Freeman pioneered and popularized this procedure, in which the doctor drove an instrument—initially an icepick, later a specialized tool called an orbitoclast—into his patients' eye sockets, separating the prefrontal cortex from the rest of the brain. His youngest patient, Howard Dully, was referred by his stepmother for the following reasons: "He objects to going to bed but then sleeps well. He does a good deal of daydreaming and when asked about it he says 'I don't know.'"

Wordsworth in the Sierra uses three lines from the 1805 version of *The Prelude.*

Sarcophagus quotes John Muir and references Muir's metaphysical discussion about the relation of man to his environment, which can be summed up in the following sentence: "The world, we are told, was made especially for man—a presumption not supported by all the facts."

photo by Agnes Magyari

Andrew Allport holds a Ph.D. in Literature and Creative Writing
from the University of Southern California. He is the author of a
chapbook, *The Ice Ship & Other Vessels*, which won the 2008
Proem Press award. His writing has appeared in numerous
national journals, including *The Antioch Review*, *Colorado Review*,
Denver Quarterly and *Boston Review*, and has been nominated
for a Pushcart Prize. He lives in Culver City, California.

The New Issues Poetry Prize

Andrew Allport, *the body | of space | in the shape of the human*
2011 Judge: David Wojahn

Jeff Hoffman, *Journal of American Foreign Policy*
2010 Judge: Linda Gregerson

Judy Halebsky, *Sky=Empty*
2009 Judge: Marvin Bell

Justin Marks, *A Million in Prizes*
2008 Judge: Carl Phillips

Sandra Beasley, *Theories of Falling*
2007 Judge: Marie Howe

Jason Bredle, *Standing in Line for the Beast*
2006 Judge: Barbara Hamby

Katie Peterson, *This One Tree*
2005 Judge: William Olsen

Kevin Boyle, *A Home for Wayward Girls*
2004 Judge: Rodney Jones

Matthew Thorburn, *Subject to Change*
2003 Judge: Brenda Hillman

Paul Guest, *The Resurrection of the Body and the Ruin of the World*
2002 Judge: Campbell McGrath

Sarah Mangold, *Household Mechanics*
2001 Judge: C.D. Wright

Elizabeth Powell, *The Republic of Self*
2000 Judge: C.K. Williams

Joy Manesiotis, *They Sing to Her Bones*
1999 Judge: Marianne Boruch

Malena Mörling, *Ocean Avenue*
1998 Judge: Philip Levine

Marsha de la O, *Black Hope*
1997 Judge: Chase Twichell